"Magic Celtic"

"Sectional Designing, Speedy Sewing"

by

Angela Madden

Acknowledgements

Very grateful thanks are due to the following.....

"Peartree Quilters" for advice and support, especially Brenda Scholes. Jane Ploughman for proof reading.

"The Maddening Crowd" Quilters for being the 'guinea pigs' in my experiments.

Eileen Flahive Daly of Clounmellane Co. Kerry for her research assistance into Celtic history and mythology.

Mary Flahive Daly of Knocknagree Co. Cork for her assistance and advice on location photography.

Alan Smith and Martin McDonald for technical advice.

Credits

Book design photography + illustration .... Angela Madden

Editor .... Theresa Wonnet

Magic Celtic © 1994 Angela Madden
ISBN 0 9521060 1 9
First Edition 1994

M. C. Q. Publications
19 Barlings Road
Harpenden, Herts
AL5 2AL England

Contents

Introduction 1

Multi-Sectional Design 4

Circle Size 5

Designing with 'Doodles' 6

Linking Sections 9

Unlinked Sectional Patterns 9

Turning 'Doodles' into 'Cords' 10

'Believable' Cords 11

Adding Overs and Unders 12

Drafting Slices 13

Understanding the 'Circle Slice' Ruler 13

Designing on the Slice 15

Completing the Design 16

Further Steps for Confident Designers 18

Transferring Designs to Fabric 20

Needleworking the Designs 23

Cutting Fabric 28

Appliqué 29

Bibliography 30

Design Placement Guide 31

Patterns 32

Twelve Page Colour Section .... Unnumbered

Introduction

Nearly a year has already passed since the publication of my first book 'Sew Easy Celtic' and thankfully the positive response has been wonderful.

Once 'Celtomania' strikes, the urge to continue can become very addictive, especially when prospective designers discover just how easy it really can be.

'Magic Celtic' is another variation using a similar process but extending the possibilities. If you're already 'hooked' you will find it an easy skill to add to your repertoire. If a novice designer you will be able to produce designs of amazing complexity after just a little practice. Either way, success is built in and the creation of unique designs, with fun and satisfaction along the way, is guaranteed.

Why 'Magic Celtic'?

This title chose itself for several reasons....

1. This design method quickly transforms anyone who uses it, with or without the possession of artistic ability, into the creator of complex circles, stars, rings, borders and scallops.

2. Circles form the basis of this method and they held great magical significance for the Celts.

3. Endless ' designer originals' can be created.

4. Circular patterns containing any number of segments can be produced in any size ...... from a greeting card design to a whole quilt top.

5. The design can change its appearance by putting colours in different places. Celtic stories are full of magical changes of appearance.

6. No mathematical or geometric calculations need be involved if the 'Circle Slice' ruler (designed to accompany this book), is put to use.

So.......Put your doubts aside for the moment......forget your lack of confidence ...... give it a try.

Think Positive .... what if you could create your own designs?..... wouldn't that be great?...... wouldn't that be Magic?

Requirements ... for designing

1. Greaseproof or thin tracing paper.
2. A fine line pencil
3. A soft eraser
4. A medium tipped black felt pen.
5. Scrap paper
6. Scissors
7. A drawing pin
8. The 'Circle Slice' Ruler

For Needleworking

1. A rotary cutter .. ruler ... cutting board
2. Bondaweb™ fusible webbing
3. An embroidery transfer pencil
4. 100% cotton plain and patterned fabrics
5. A small flat sided magnet

Circular patterns created from repeated wedge - shaped sections produce fascinating Celtic-Knotwork designs. From Iron Age artefacts to present day greeting cards, their popularity has endured. Similar patterns appear in many other cultures worldwide.

Many famous artists have played with this design concept and produced intricate patterns. Two of the best known were originally constructed for craftworkers by Leonardo Da Vinci and Albrect Dürer. They are shown below. Their designs have been much admired, but it has proved to be beyond the capabilities of the average person to produce similar patterns without resorting to a photocopier and exact reproductions.

It is a certainty that I am no 'Leonardo', neither do I know how he went about creating his design. However, I do know that anyone can now produce similar but original ones with a little practice. The applications for craftworkers in general and appliqué, embroidery and quilting in particular are endless.

Albrect Dürer's "Sechs Knoten"

A Magic Celtic Design

Leonardo Da Vinci's "Concatenation"

Space for one of your designs!

Before we start.....a few points

1. Celtic Knotwork appears to be constructed from cords which have neither beginning nor end. They travel along passing alternately over and under every other cord they meet.

2. The name derives from the loose knots which are created forming complex but ordered designs. Spaces existing between cords are decorated with filler patterns.

3. Knotwork designs can be constructed using any number of cords. Some of these may be very long and travel around the whole area covered by the pattern. Others may be short and present only a small section.

4. Separate design units which do not interlink with each other can also be used to make sectional patterns.

5. Cords cross each other one at a time. This makes the interweaving very clear to understand. They never cross each other in 'bunches' or run along on top of one another.

6. There is usually symmetry in completed designs, but the individual repeated sections may be asymmetrical.

7. Colour in designs can be provided by the cords themselves.....the spaces between them......or a combination of both. A single cord can change colour as it progresses throughout the design.

8. This style of Celtic designing is based upon drawing doodles and not academic art. Early designs will be entirely the result of chance. There will be marvellous surprises, when a simple scribble can be transformed into a fascinating complex pattern.

9. A little practice and experimentation will enable patterns to be planned, controlled and manipulated to suit requirements.

10. From the first attempt onwards, all designs will work perfectly if the instructions are carefully followed. The principles are not difficult and will be quickly absorbed, then the fun starts!

11. Although circles are the main 'building block' of these designs, the finished result need not necessarily be round. This applies particularly to patterns with few sections.

A Look at Multi-Sectional Circular Designs

Before we put pencil to paper it is worth spending a short time looking at circles and their possibilities. By considering a circle as though it were a pie about to be sliced, it is very easy to see that this can be achieved in a number of ways.

Assuming that everyone to be served wanted an equal sized piece, the size of the slice they received would vary according to the number of people being served. If there were only two people they would each receive half a pie. If there were ten people they would get a very much smaller slice.

The amount of pie contained in any particular slice would depend on the overall size of the pie. Small pies yield short slices, whilst large pies would provide longer ones and therefore more pastry surface to decorate with cream.

All this directly applies to circular designs created from slices. Study the following examples contained varying numbers of equal sized slices.

A five slice design

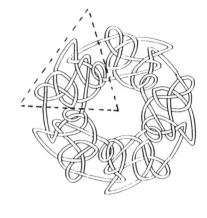

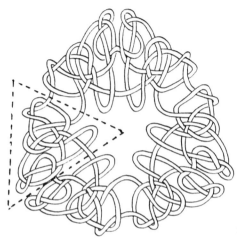
A six slice design

a seven slice design

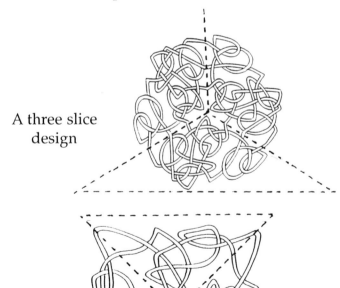
A three slice design

A four slice design

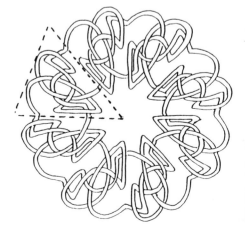
An eight slice design

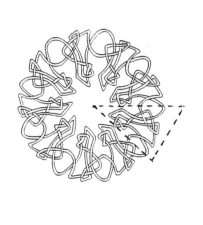

A nine slice design

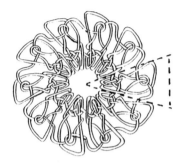

A ten slice design

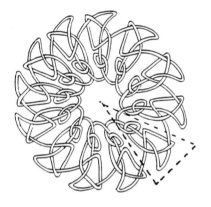

A twelve slice design

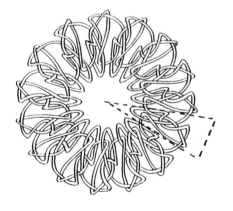

A fifteen slice design

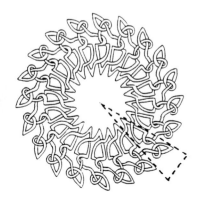

A twenty slice design

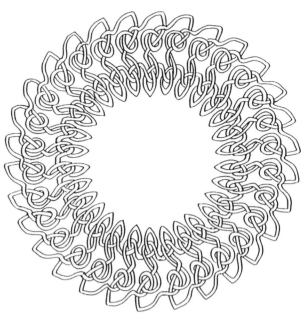

A thirty slice design

In theory any number of slices can be used when designing . The preceding divisions are those I have found to be of most use.

The size of the Circle

It is important from the outset to consider the overall size of any proposed design in conjunction with the intended number of slices.

When using smaller circles eg. 8 ins or 12 ins coupled with a high number of slices, eg. 10 or 12, the slice surface will be short and narrow. This will enforce the use of a simpler design, or one in which the elements are very close together, in order for them to fit into the space.

This does not imply however that a single section containing a simple pattern will not look attractive and complex when repeated around the circle.

Circles with a larger diameter can accommodate a greater number of slices. They can contain more complex designs and a greater number of cords, since each piece will be both longer and wider at the outer edge, affording more design space.

For the purpose of design practice, begin by using 12 in circles with between 3 and 8 slices. This will provide a good balance between the size of the individual pattern elements and overall complexity. Almost all the examples photographed in this book lie within this size range.

Tip.... should you ever wish to create a very small design (eg. a 2 in or less diameter circle) it can be easily achieved by creating a larger design which can be reduced by means of a photocopier. This process will also reduce any imperfections in the drawing and improve the overall appearance. The reduced design will however contain cords which may be too minute for needlework applications. They are most suitable as impressive original logos or embellishments for notepaper, cards etc. Never attempt to draw designs this tiny ...... it may lead to insanity!

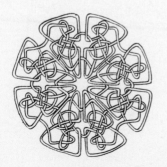

Designing with Doodles

This style of designing begins with simple loopy doodles .... be confident, it is not advanced art!

Relax have fun experiment without thinking too deeply about these squiggles and where they should go. Deep thought on this subject will only hold your progress back, since you do not know how to control designs at this stage.

> **Remember**..... In this method leaving everything to chance will produce great patterns from the start despite all your doubts.... this is magic.

Practice Exercise

1. Try out the following principles first on scrap paper using pencil (For the moment forget all about slices.)

2. All knotwork designs are basically made up of loops and curves.

Aim to draw rounded 'well-fed' loops, the tops of which can be curved or pointed as you wish. Avoid tiny tight loops and also long thin ones. When loops close, the crossing lines should be as near to a right angle as possible.

3. All loops must be 'tied into' the design by means of another cord passing through them........as if threading a bead.

4. Practice looping doodles into circular shapes, then threading second doodles through all loops.

5. Avoid creating 'lonely loops' which are not connected into the design by another line. The exception to this rule might possibly be at the outside edge of designs.

Such loops can create agreeable patterns............

but they have the effect of simplifying the design, removing the enticement to follow a cord around, with your eyes discovering where it goes. 'Lonely loops' can be understood at a glance and do not hold the interest and attention of the observer.

> **Remember**........ Knotwork needs to be knotted...............if there are no knots, it's not Knotwork!

6. Each cord only crosses one other cord at every crossing point throughout the design. This enables the weaving over and under to be clearly understood. There are never places at which a 'spaghetti junction' develops with several cords on top of each other. These would be 'confused crossings'.

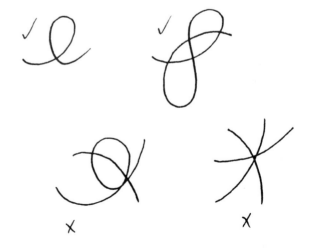

7. All of the designs we will be producing will be on pie slice shaped sections. The placement of doodles on these sections will effect the completed design.

For initial practice purposes use randomly drawn triangular shapes.

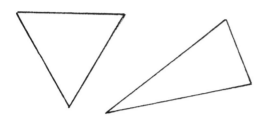

8. Long cords which travel all the way around a design always enter at one side of a slice and after doodling around in the middle they always exit on the opposite side.

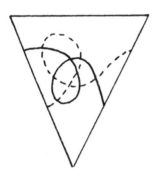

9. Doodling across the wide end of a slice will produce a ring design with a blank centre.

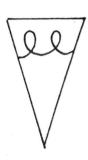 

10. Doodling over the whole area of a slice will produce a completely filled circular design.

 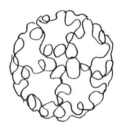

11. Leaving areas of the slice blank will produce spaces in the filled circular design (see front cover photograph)

Shapes can be drawn onto the slice before doodling commences. Care must be taken when doing this to allow room for the doodles to pass around them.

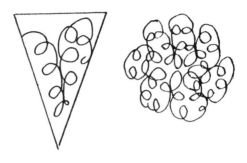

Leaving such spaces within designs can widen the needlework options, as they can be filled with quilting, patchwork, embroidery or appliqué to compliment and enhance the knotwork.

Linking Sections Together

1. In order to complete the circular design correctly it is vital that each slice connects in a continuous way with both of its neighbours. This is achieved by making matched registration points along the sides of the slice, where cords enter and exit.

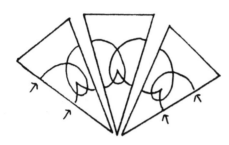

2. As long as the same number of registration points occur in matching positions, the sides of the slices will link correctly. This will happen when identical patterns are repeated and also when different ones are alternated.

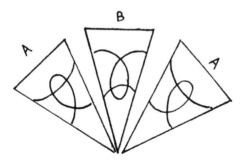

However alternating patterns will only work successfully when an even number of slices are included in a design.

Unlinked Sectional Patterns

Complex sectional patterns can also be constructed from separate, self-contained units between which no links occur. Cords remain and are complete within each unit. Triangular shapes have many possibilities in addition to forming circles and can make useful border designs.

The design doodles in these separate units do not enter or exit the sections. Instead they 'float' in the centre of the unit shape. Each doodled line must be complete and continuous within the unit like an 'elastic band.'

> **Tip**........if a symmetrical, unlinked unit design is required, the easiest way to achieve this is by folding the unit shape in half. If this is done using greaseproof paper the half doodle can be drawn, then traced on the other side to complete the design.

Turning Doodles into 'Cords'

1. Each doodle drawn so far represents one side of a cord. It is necessary to draw the other side to get a clear view of the design and eliminate any possible spacing problems. This is called 'doubling' up.

2. Before attempting to do this consider the width of the cords you have in mind.........

   a) <u>For machine Embroidery</u> or <u>Quilting designs</u>....... any width is possible. Thin cords around wide spaces, or fat cords around small spaces both work well.

   b) <u>For Bias Appliqué</u>..... the width of the bias fabric used will be controlled by the width of the bias bars available. These are thin strips of metal or polyester specially made to aid pressing bias for appliqué. Their method of use is explained later and they are made in several sizes. For practice in design, 1/4in is a good size to choose, as it looks attractive in cushion or quilt block sized designs.

   When this decision of size is made, the 'doubled up' cords you create in your design must match this chosen bar width. If it does not, it may not be possible to needlework the design without encountering spacing problems.

3. 'Doubling up' in a doodle is easy. Simply draw another line alongside and parallel to the first at the chosen distance away.

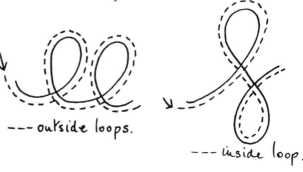

--- outside loops.

--- inside loop.

4. Ignore 'overs and unders' for the present. Draw through all cord crossings.

5. Notice how the second line always travels on the same side of loops which face in the same direction, and visa versa.

6. Notice also how 'doubling up' on the outside of a loop increases its overall size, by invading the surrounding space. Loops doubled up on the inside become smaller.

7. It is easy to alter the proportions of any doodled design by manipulating which side of loops and curves it will be best to double up on. Change over to the other side of a line if you wish. Do this on a convenient section of line, then repair the cord outline. This is called a 'switch'.

repair

switch

8. At times the choice of which side of a line you can double upon, will be made for you. Due to lack of space between existing lines, doubling up on one side may be impossible, and you are forced to switch in order to continue.

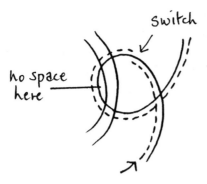

switch

no space here

9. Watch out for places where more than two cords cross close together. Remember the rule that one cord can only cross one other at a time.

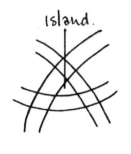

Island.

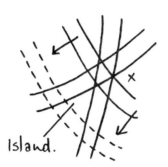

Island.

Notice how a small island exists between three cords which cross each other in close proximity. A 'build up' of cords on top of each other will never be clear and needs to be eliminated by spacing them out to create an island.

10. When the drawn doubled lines need to be perfectly spaced apart (eg when these lines are to be used as a guide for machine embroidery or quilting) a simple trick will enable you to create perfect parallel lines.

> **Tip**..... tape two pencil together and use one to follow the first doodled line while the second creates the new perfectly spaced line. Widen the distance between pencils to create a wider cord. Tape a cocktail stick to a pencil to produce a narrow one.

The above is unnecessary when designing for bias appliqué as your doodled lines will not be transferred to the fabric.

Creating 'Believable' Cords

1. Whatever the chosen cord width, do check all crossing points to make sure the cords are believable. This means that as they cross each other they look continuous and not severed and displaced.

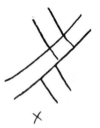

Displacement usually occurs when a little erasing of lines has taken place, resulting in parts of a doodle being moved, or when the doubling up line changes sides without a repair having been made to the cord outline.

2. Displacement can also occur at the registration points. A very good practice to adopt is that of always making the registration point fall in the centre of a cord rather than at one edge.

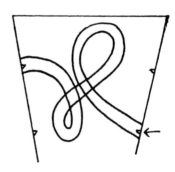

3. When all doubling up has been completed in pencil, go over the cord lines in black felt tipped pen......

EXCEPT for where lines cross each other. Leave the centres of all crossing cords blank.

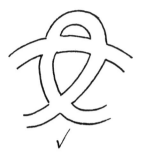

✓   ✗

> **Help!**.... should you mistakenly go through the centre of crossing cords, typists correction fluid will save the day.

4.   Erase all pencil lines at the centres of crossing cords.

Adding 'Overs and Unders'

1.   Return to using pencil.......

   a) <u>Unlinked sectional designs</u>
   begin at any crossing point, marking it clearly with an arrow outside the cord to indicate the starting point.

   b) <u>Linked slice designs</u>
   begin at the entry point of any cord at the side of a slice........

   and..... follow one cord to the next place at which it crosses another.

Decide if the cord you have chosen to follow will pass over or under the other. Draw in the sides of whichever cord lies on top as if you were drawing the side rails of a bridge.

2.   Continue to follow the same cord to the next crossing, where it will pass in the opposite way, once again mark the sides of the cord which lies on top.

   You will alternately be drawing.....

   as you progress around the design.

3.   Do not miss out any crossings.

4.   When the first cord has been followed to its end, (either the starting point arrow, or the exit point at the side of the slice) look out for any unmarked crossings. These will occur if the cord you haven't been following crosses itself, or in designs containing more than two cords, where all the other cords cross. Take your cue from neighbouring marked crossings and complete the interweaving correctly.

5. Completed designs should always interweave correctly at the point where the end meets the start. This applies equally to the short cords in unlinked sectional designs and to long cords which interweave throughout linked multisectional patterns.

6. Partial designs have no foolproof way of being checked for mistakes on a single slice. A few minutes spent repeating the well known ancient Celtic chant of......

   "over, under, over, under," or its alternative version......

   "under, over, under, over," as you check each crossing should do the trick.

   (The chorus to this chant, well known to Celtic design workshops, is "shut up", addressed to neighbours who are loudly going 'over', when you are going 'under'!)

   > **Remember** .....any mistakes in the crossings in a slice will be duplicated all around the completed design. Time spent checking, is time well spent.

Creating Accurate Slices

In order to create a circular design which lies flat and in which all slices fit correctly, it is essential that two things are accurate.
1. That the angle at the point of the slice is drawn correctly for the intended number of repeats.
2. That all repeated slices are equal in size.

Drafting Slices

The correct angle forming the pointed end of a slice, enabling it to meet its' neighbours at the centre of the circle will be.......

   360° ÷ the intended number of slices

   eg.

   360° ÷ 5 = 72° angle for a five segment circle.

Any angles can of course be correctly drafted using a protractor... but if your maths and eye sight are anything like mine, using the 'Circle Slice' ruler created for this purpose is a lot faster, easier and more accurate.

Understanding the 'Circle Slice' Ruler

Study the rule markings carefully.

1. The circled numbers enable you to choose the number of slices you wish to include in the completed design. (For a first attempt use ⑥ i.e. six slices).

2. The numbered inches along the right hand edge allow you to choose the size of circle you wish to create. The figures increase in 2in jumps, referring to the diameter, while the distance between them is only 1in, referring to the radius. (For a first attempt use the figure 12, for a 12 in diameter circle suitable for a block).

3. The * line extending from ④ to the right hand rulers edge indicates the centre of the circle at its extreme right hand tip. (If the ruler were to be pivoted around in a circle this would be the pivotal point.)

To use the 'Circle Slice'

1. Select the circled number corresponding with the number of slices you intend to use in you design.

2. Place the line running through this circled number exactly on top of the left hand edge of a sheet of scrap paper.

3. Check that the papers' edge is also lying directly under the centre of the *

4. Using a fine lead pencil, draw a line along the ruler's right hand side from the paper's edge to the required circle diameter figure.

5. Without changing the ruler's position, slide it back slightly, enabling the tip of the * line to meet the paper's edge.

6. Mark the size of the chosen circle on the pencil line.

7. Realign the ruler's right hand side so that it butts up to the paper's edge, with the * line meeting the point where the pencil line reaches the edge of the paper. Mark the same chosen size of circle on the paper's edge.

The angled end of the slice is now correct and complete. The way in which the two circle size marks are linked will control the shape of the wider end of the slice.

Consider the following alternatives.........

a) Linking them with a straight line will give a flat sided circle.

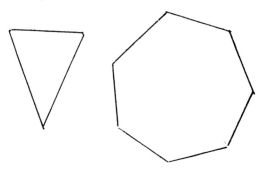

b) Linking them with a curve will produce a round or scalloped edge.

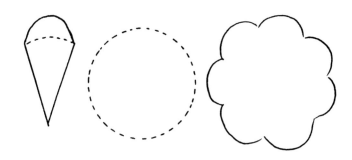

c) Linking them with an angled line will produce 'star points' around the circle.

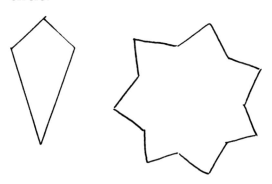

Tip..... the easiest way to achieve b) and c) above is to cut the slice out accurately along the pencil line allowing extra paper at the wider end. Fold the slice in half lengthwise and trim the wide end to the desire shape with scissors.

Making Side Registration Points:

1. Cut out and fold the slice as just described, if you haven't already done so.

2. Snip through both sides together with scissors, to produce matched position registration points. The number of snips must correspond with the number of cords to be included. (For practice purposes, until confident use 2 cords and therefore 2 registration point snips.

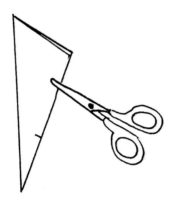

Remember.... These snips will be the CENTRE of the cords as they enter and exit the slice.

Designing on the Slice

1. Unfold the slice.

2. Mark the chosen width of the cords at the registration point snips (for practice using 1/4in cords, the markings will therefore be 1/8 in either side of all snips.)

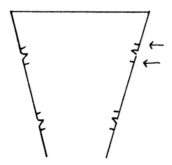

3. Lightly draw your first doodle design line, starting from one of the side cord markings. Meander around the slice, creating loops and curves as you wish (for practice use two loops maximum. Once confident use as many as you wish) Exit at the opposite side of the slice at an equivalent mark. If you started at a mark above a snip, end at one above a snip and visa versa.

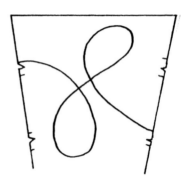

As the diagram shows it is not necessary to go from the top left snip to the top right snip, but you could if you wanted to.

4. Draw the second design doodle as above joining the vacant snip markings. Watch out for lonely loops.

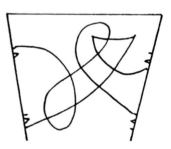

5. Double up these lines and complete the over/under interweaving as previously explained.

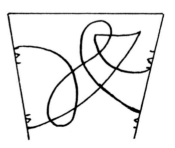

All landscape photographs are of Co. Kerry in the South West of Ireland. An area of outstanding beauty, it has strong direct links in language, culture and the ancestry of its population with the ancient Celts.

Kerry Coastline, a view little changed since Celtic times.

Circling clockwise, or 'sunwise', held a special significance for the Celts. Dancing in this way called 'Deisiol', kept the sun on course, aiding both fertility of crops and safety in battle.

Spinning star (Pattern p.33)
A magical design .... turn to next page to see why....

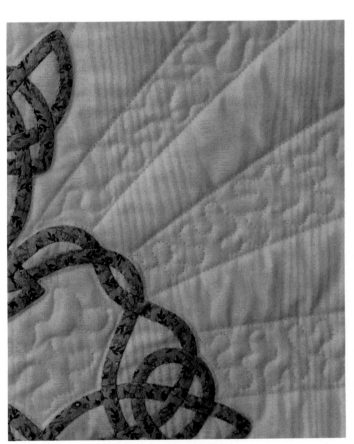

Detail showing vermicelli quilting.

Spinning Star changes its appearance .....
(a phenomenon common in Celtic tales.
Gods, Godesses and sacred animals could
take numerous shapes and names)

The Gap of Dunloe, Killarney.

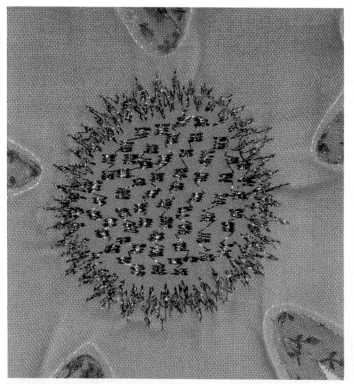

Detail of flower centre above ..... showing satin
stitch beads and peaky straight stitch (p. 25,26)

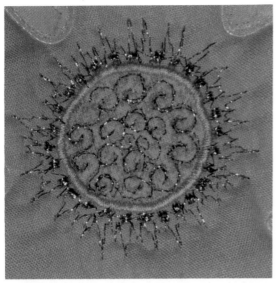

Detail of flower centre showing a combination
of free straight stitch, p. 26, irregular zig zag,
p. 25, and satin stitch beads, p. 25.

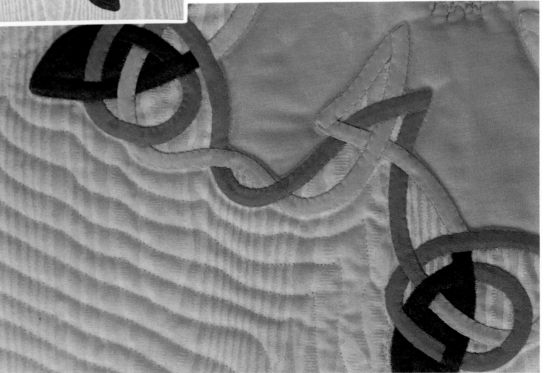

Under the old bridge at Inch.

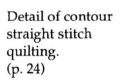

Detail of contour
straight stitch
quilting.
(p. 24)

Forest Flower (Pattern p. 33)

The Celts venerated holy trees and through them ancient local gods, (now disguised as Christian Saints of often dubious origin). The 5th century Christian Council of Arles denounced 'those who offer vows to trees, wells or stones.'
Celtic chieftains were often crowned beneath special trees.

Detail of flower centre which has been slightly padded. The irregular zig zag stitching, p. 25, serves to cover the edges of the appliqued green fabric.

Fairy Ring (pattern p. 32)

The woods around Killarney.

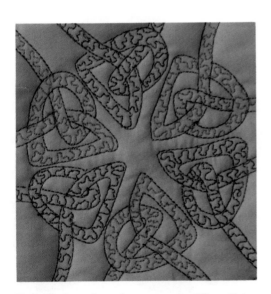

Detail showing tiny vermicelli quilting
providing colour inside the design
cords.

Bridge near Carah Lake.

Forest flower design changes its appearance.

Unlinked sectional designs.

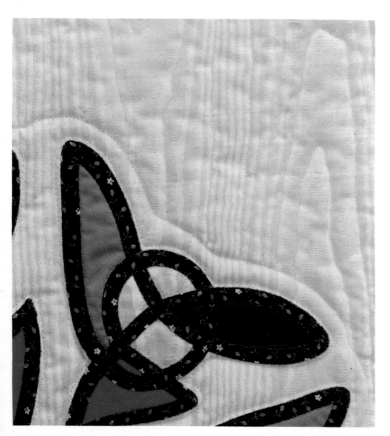

Detail showing straight stitched quilting using pattern on fabric as a guide.

The Gap of Dunloe, Killarney.

The whitethorn tree was special, a favourite of the 'little people', 'good people' or 'fairies' ....
but beware they could turn nasty if crossed!

Magic Celtic Wallhanging ..... details.

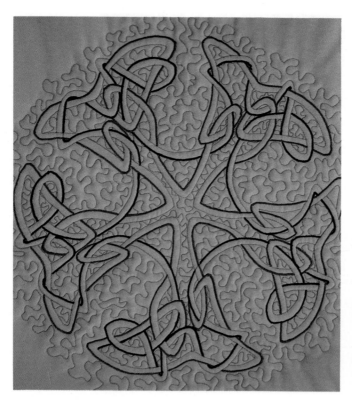

Celtic Tranquility

Dusk at a Killarney Lake

Detail showing vermicelli stitching and satin stitch p.25 used to quilt and embroider at the same time.

Star of the Sea :

Detail showing
irregular zig zag used
as a filler stitch (p. 25)

At his death King Feradhach divided his
Kingdom, Ireland. The first son got all of the
wealth and treasure, cattle herds, castles and forts.
The younger got the seashore, cliffs, food of the
woods and sea, salmon and game.
The Celts considered the second son better off
since he could move around with the breeze, the
earth providing for his needs, while his brother
had to remain in one place tending his cattle and property.

Minard Castle.

Tartan Star
Appliquéd only, to be quilted

Wild fuchsia abounds in the Autumn.

Detail. Small tartans work beautifully for bias appliqué.

Caherconree.... the most notable inland, Celtic promontory fort in Ireland. Guarded on three sides by sheer cliffs, it was believed to spin at terrific speed when the sun set.

Celtic Sun Wallhanging (unfinished)

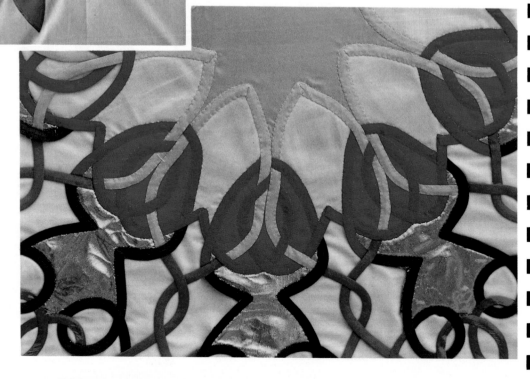

Detail

Linking up......
Completing the Design

Try out all new brand pens........

If your pen does not transfer......
Forget that I raised the subject!

If your pen does transfer ..... either

1. Find another to use.......or

2. Use it, but ensure that the side of the greaseproof paper on which the design is completed is not placed next to the fabric during the later stage of transferring the design.

Method:

1. Take a sheet of greaseproof paper large enough to accommodate the completed design. (The practice design needs a minimum of 12 in square.)

When confident you may wish to produce very large designs eg., a whole quilt top. For this, tape several sheets of greaseproof paper together, completing the design on the untaped side.

2. Fold the paper into four, to find the centre point.

3. To facilitate easy linking between sections, a drawing pin is a valuable aid. In order to make this pin easier to handle (and find!) .... cut a small circle of coloured plastic (approx 1 in diameter). The flat end of an aerosol can lid is ideal. Pierce this plastic disc centrally with the drawing pin.

4. Circular patterns can be assembled with perfectly fitting sections, if the slice containing the design can be pivoted around and repeatedly traced. However, it is not possible to simply stick a pin into the slice itself as the pivot, since the actual centre of the design is situated at the extreme tip of the slice point.

It is therefore necessary to extend this point by sticking a tab of folded, clear sticky tape onto the slice. This enables the point to be clearly seen and the tab of tape to be pierced, at the slices extreme tip. Insert the drawing pin from the underside of the slice. You may wish to put another piece of tape on top of the tab to strengthen it and prevent the hole from tearing.

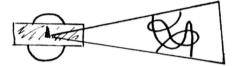

5. Turn to P31 and select the appropriate design placement guide, which contains the same number of sections as you wish to create.

6. Place the centre of the greaseproof paper directly over this guide. Trace the radiating spokes accurately.

   (This guide will aid even spacing of slices around the circle, lessening the chance of overlaps, or gaps occurring, it will also provide a means of checking the accuracy of your cut out slice.) Stick a piece of clear tape over the guide centre on the back of the paper to reinforce it.

7. Pierce the centre of the traced design guide with a pin, and place this hole on top of the upturned drawing pin, which already pierces the slice tab once again the clear tape will protect the pin hole from tearing.

8. Press your eraser on top of the pin, to lock the papers in position, and prevent you from inadvertently spearing yourself.

9. It will now be possible to rotate the design slice around under the greaseproof paper. This will enable repeated tracings to be made in each section between the design guide spokes.

10. Carefully compare the sides of the slice with one section of the traced design guide. If the cut sides exactly match the drawn spokes....wonderful.

    But if ....

    a) the design slice is wider.... trim both sides of the slice equally to the correct size.

    b) the design slice is narrower..... position it exactly centrally between spokes for each tracing. The gaps will be eliminated by slightly extending the cords each time at both sides.

11. Accurately trace the design slice in each section until the circle has been completed. The finished design is now ready to be transferred to the background fabric.

    The interweaving of cords will have taken care of itself as you progressed and will be correct throughout, if it was correct on the design slice.

    All designs are unique and the mind-boggling complexity is easily achieved....as if by magic.

Further Steps for Confident Designers

Symmetry in Design

Multi-sliced designs can be created from individual slices which contain either a symmetrical or asymmetrical pattern.

A ten slice design made up from repeating an asymmetrical slice would look like this:

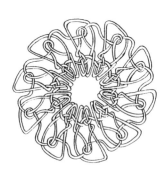

Designs produced from such asymmetrical slices often create the impression of movement. They are exciting, interesting circles which appear to spin 'Catherine Wheel' style due to the way in which the segments link.

Many designs of this type suggest flower shapes and this likeness can be enhanced by the addition of a flower centre to the design (see second page of colour section)

A six slice design made from symmetrical slices would look like this

(A six slice symmetrical design is also a twelve slice asymmetrical design)

Circles produced from symmetrical slices appear static. They are pleasing due to their more predictable, classic regularity. They have a more traditional look about them.

Using Odd and Even Numbers of design slices

Both odd and even numbers of design sections will work well. There are however a few points worth considering before proceeding to experiment.

1. Odd numbered designs containing asymmetrical slices will only work if each individual slice is rotated around the circle, facing the same direction each time it repeats.

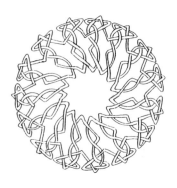

The finished effect is then a whole design which flows around, as its' slices combine.

2. Even numbered designs using asymmetric slices can of course rotate in an identical way.

    However, in addition it is possible to flip each slice over and thereby produce its'mirror image, to be used in alternate sections around the design. This is the way to produce symmetrical slices which are in reality double asymmetrical slices. It is therefore possible to produce two different but related designs from the original design slice. (see following diagram.)

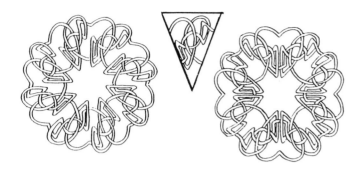

Using Short Cords:

As mentioned earlier, it is possible to use short cords in designs. In fact the whole pattern can be made up from linking them together. They can also be mixed in with long cords.

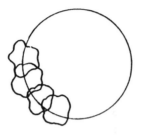

These short cords do not travel all around the design, so do not cross design slices like long cords. Instead they enter and exit on the same side.

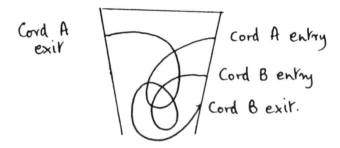

In the above example, cord A will travel all around the design, while cord B will only be repeated on one side of the slice. It will therefore need to be placed beside a matched slice to maintain continuity. Such designs will therefore need to be constructed from an even number of slices, to be successfully joined up.

The registration points on the short cord side will always need to accommodate the extra exit point.

The matched neighbouring slice can be an exact mirror image which will produce a symmetrical short cord. Alternatively a

Creating Symmetrical Slices:

1. This is achieved by tracing the design slice in **every other** space between the spokes. Leave the alternative spaces blank.

2. Turn the greaseproof paper over so that you are now tracing on the reverse side. (Remember the felt pen warning on P16)

3. Trace the design slice again in the missing sections. It will now be turned the other way round. DO NOT trace the over's and under s on these reversed sections. Leave all intersections blank.

4. Mark these intersections correctly from the right side when all the tracing is complete.

Mixing Slices:

If registration points match, it is possible to mix different but equal sized design slices to widen the artistic possibilities.

This principle of mixing slices applies to both symmetrical and asymmetrical design slices.... but will of course only succeed with even numbered designs if they alternate.

matching but different neighbouring slice can be used as described in 'Mixing Slices'.

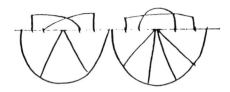

Creating Borders with Half Circles

The principle of producing circular Knotwork designs can be modified to create lovely scalloped border designs. These can be made from using half circles, so only even numbered segment designs (which can be divided) can be used.

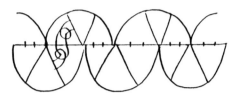

The half circles are created in the usual way and the cords which exit along the exposed straight side can be ended off in many ways.

Unlinked sectional designs also work well ....

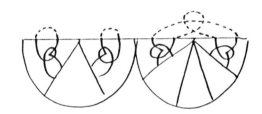

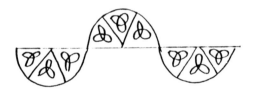

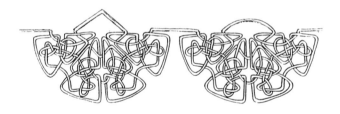

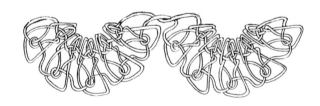

Transferring Designs to Fabric

Once the completed design is ready, the method of transferring it onto the backing fabric will depend on the way in which it is to be needleworked.

Machine Embroidery or Quilting

This requires a double outline as perfectly drawn as is possible, to provide a stitching guide. There are two possible ways of acquiring this......

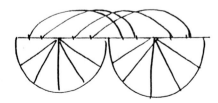

1.   Pin or tack the top fabric, wadding and backing fabric together..... pin the

paper design on top and stitch through both paper and fabric. The perforations produced by the needle will enable the paper to be torn away with ease. Any stubborn paper which remains can be removed with tweezers, or by soaking for a few minutes in water. This is my preferred method for outlining cords in small designs, however do not try to embroider areas between cords with filler stitches before the paper has been removed.

2. Trace the double outline through the fabric using a light box, with one of the following......

a)   A fine lead pencil....lightly drawn lines will disappear under the stitching.

b)   A fine coloured pencil..... matching the thread colour.

c)   A white pencil or chalk..... for use on dark fabric.

d)   A light erasable or water soluble pen...... but be aware that both have the capacity to alter the fabric colour due to their chemical composition and the long term effects on particular fabrics are unknown, unless totally removed by washing.

Bias Appliquéd Designs

My preferred method of design transfer for this technique is by means of an embroidery transfer pencil. This is unsuitable for use with both embroidery or quilting designs as pencils vary in their capacity to be removed by washing. It is wise to always assume that they are permanent markers. The bias applique cords will cover the marks completely.

Embroidery transfer pencils are readily available in several colours suitable for marking light and medium coloured fabrics. A white transfer pen will soon be available for marking dark fabrics.

These pencils are designed to be used on paper. The markings will then transfer to fabric when moderate heat is applied, using an iron.

> **Tip**.... it is advantageous to use these pencils against a hard, unyielding surface. This enables a heavy line to be drawn, ensuring that multiple transfers are possible from the same design.

Avoiding Transferring Problems:

1. A single line drawn centrally along each cord between the double lines is sufficient to indicate the placement position of bias cords. A continuous line at a crossing indicates an 'over' cord and a broken one, an 'under'.

> **Remember**..... to use the transfer pencil on the reverse side of the paper from the felt pen, if it also transfers.

2. Transfer pencils can easily be accidentally smeared around the design if rubbed. The smear will mark the backing cloth when ironed so is best avoided. This can be easily done by using an extended little finger as a supporting prop, enabling the whole hand to be held clear of the paper while you are drawing. (Hold the pencil in the normal way, stick your

little finger out straight. Put the tip of your little finger on the paper between transfer markings and without letting the rest of you hand touch the paper continue drawing. Your outstretched finger will help you to be stable and prevent 'wobbles.')

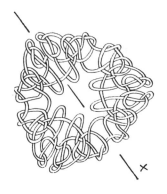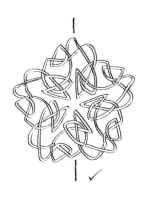

3. A few pencils become very runny when heated, especially dark blue ones. To protect your ironing board cover from an unexpected Celtic decoration, shield it with paper before transferring begins. The majority of pencils do not however require this precaution.

Successful Transfer

1. Celtic designs can be more clearly seen against plain background fabrics. Patterned fabrics tend to confuse the eye and compete with the design, Infill colours or embroidered designs in the spaces can be used as embellishment to liven up the plain background.

2. Beginners should choose a light coloured background since transfer pencil markings will show up very clearly against it.

3. Laundered fabric accepts transferred markings more easily.

4. Fold the chosen size background fabric into quarters, lightly pressing the folds to mark the centre and facilitate correct design placement.

5. For all designs... especially those containing an odd number of segments, do find the most pleasing placement of the design before pinning. Asymmetrical or odd numbered designs can look 'skewed' in a careless position and wonderful when more thoughtfully placed.

6. Place the greaseproof paper with the transfer pencil marked side next to the fabric.

7. Pin through the centres of both paper and fabric.

8. Pin the corners and side mid-points of the paper. Remove the central pin.

9. Transfer the design using a moderately hot dry iron, using a 'press and wait' technique, rather than ironing it, It surprises many that the transfer may take a little time. Turn the iron around in case the sole plate does not heat to a uniform temperature throughout.

10 When checking that the design has transferred, remove only one pin at a time to prevent the paper shifting. When you are certain that a good quality transfer is complete remove the paper.

Food for Thought

It is possible to use the transfer pencil on the design slice itself. This could then be rotated and repeatedly transferred to complete the design, either onto paper or fabric.

It would seem that both time and effort could then be saved, eliminating all tracing. However, be warned that there would be a far greater possibility of problems with spacing the sections. Once transferred, placement mistakes could not be remedied.

The full, completed design could not be appreciated and evaluated without the double lines. Therefore.... unless you are confident and experienced, do not consider the tracing to be optional. It is your safeguard and will ensure success.

Needleworking the Designs

Celtic designs lend themselves beautifully to machine sewn techniques. They are speedy and good looking if well done.

Designs can be machine embroidered on single fabric held in an embroidery hoop prior to quilting. Alternatively, the same stitches can be sewn through the quilt sandwich... top, wadding and backing...decorating and quilting in a single step.

Machine embroidery, quilting and appliqué can produce high quality results in a fraction of the hand sewing time. A little effort spent in gaining mastery over your sewing machine will be very worthwhile. The following section is designed to assist in achieving that goal.

Sewing machines vary in their capacity to carry out different techniques, this section will hopefully provide a guide to the stitches I find most useful. It should be used in conjunction with your sewing machine instruction book. Do not despair if you cannot do some of the stitch techniques listed, since a normal straight stitch alone can be very effective as a means of outlining cords or appliquéing bias.

A Few General Points

1. The machine can be used in the normal way, using an ordinary foot.

   or.....

2. The moving teeth beneath the foot called the 'Feed Dog' can be lowered or covered up, and a darning foot used to produce free machine stitching.

> **Please note**.... disengaging the feed dog by lowering or covering, eliminates the machines' ability to control stitch length and direction. The sewer now controls both of these, and can move the fabric at will.

3. To achieve the best results in either embroidery or quilting, the bobbin thread tension should be tightened, (if this is possible on your machine.)

   Metallic and transparent threads benefit from having the top tension loosened off a little. The effects of both of these adjustments in tension is that the threads engage underneath the fabric and the work is not spoilt by stray bobbin thread appearing on the top.

4. Many threads work well for machine embroidery. Speciality threads are widely available, in a host of colours and special effects. However more humble threads can also produce pleasing effects and are good for practice purposes.

5. It is <u>VITAL</u> to use the correct sized needle when machine embroidering or quilting.......

   <u>Very fine</u> .....60/8.....70/10
   For embroidery and transparent thread. The holes made will be very small and inobtrusive, giving a high quality result.

   <u>Large Eyed</u>.....90/14....100/16...110/18
   For metallic threads, to eliminate the possibility of shredding during sewing, due to friction..... or....

   For enabling two threads to be sewn at the same time through one needle, for a stronger colour effect.

23

6. Be comfortable during your sewing sessions.... consider the relative height of chair, table and sewing machine.

7 Make sure your work is well lit.

8. Sit directly in front of the machine needle.

9. Use the removable extender table if your machine has one..... if not extend the machine arm surface by placing a book of equal height beside it.

10. Change position frequently...... stand up and walk around.

11. Support you arms while embroidering and quilting by.....

   a)   Supporting your wrists on the machine extender table..... or by....

   b)   Pushing the machine a little away from you and leaning your elbows on the table as you work.

12. Always do five or ten minutes practice on scrap fabric before beginning to work on your 'heirloom'.

Useful Machine Stitches to Practice:

Straight stitch: useful for straight or gently curving embroidery lines..... straight line or contour quilting.... applique stitching on bias

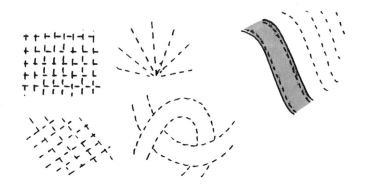

> Machine set as follows.....
> selected stitch........straight.
> stitch width ....O.
> stitch length ....optional.
> feed dog ....engaged.
> machine foot   normal/walking foot.
> speed ....as comfortable.

Method.....allow the fabric to feed normally, use the side of the machine foot as a width guide....change width by altering the needle position.

The use of a walking foot (extra to most machines) prevents gathers occurring on the reverse side of the work.

For appliqué use invisible thread in the needle. Bobbin thread should match background fabric.

Zig Zag Stitich: useful for appliqué of bias cords.

> Machine set as follows....
> selected stitch........zig zag.
> stitch width ....very narrow.
> stitich length ....very short.
> feed dog ....enagaged.
> machine foot ....normal foot.
> speed ....as comfortable.

Method...'zig' on the bias strip, 'zag' on the background fabric. Use invisible thread in the needle. Bobbin thread should match background fabric.

Satin Stitch: useful for outlining the edges of cords with definite bands of colour

Machine set as follows.....
selected stitch... zig zag.
stitch width ...... optional.
stitch length ..... almost O.
feed dog .... engaged.
machine foot .... normal/embroidery.
speed .... as comfortable.

Method.... allow fabric to feed through machine ..... don't push... stitches should be evenly placed very close together.... no gaps. Lift presser foot at intervals to allow fabric to be turned on tight curves. Always stop machine with needle in fabric and <u>on the outside edge</u> of the curve during repositioning to prevent gaps.

Irregular zig zag: useful for filling areas.... creating bands of colour.... looks especially good in variegated coloured threads.

Machine set as follows........
selected stitch.... zig zag.
stitch width .... medium to wide .
stitch length ...... irrelevant as.....
feed dog .... disengaged .
machine foot ..... darning foot.
speed .... easier at fast speed

Method..... move the fabric backwards and forwards in the required direction, producing zig zag stitches of different lengths and widths. For filling areas work backwards and forward in 'shaky' rows.

Satin Stitch Beads: useful for filling spaces... providing colour and texture..... particularly good in metallic threads.

Machine set as follows.....
selected stitch.... zig zag.
stitch width .... medium to wide.
stitch length ...... irrelevant as.......
feed dog .... disengaged.
machine foot ..... darning foot.
speed .... short fast bursts

Method..... sew approximately six or seven stitches very close together...lift needle..... move fabric slightly.....repeat stitches....move fabric........repeat. No need to cut linking thread between beads, they are so short that they hardly show at all.

Free Straight Stitch: useful for outlining irregular shapes.... creating filler designs... personalizing work with names, dates, signatures etc. either in embroidery or quilting.

Machine set as follows............
selected stitch... straight stitch.
stitch width ...... O.
stitch length ..... irrelevant as....
feed dog .... disengaged.
machine foot .... darning.
speed   as comfortable,
                  steady pace.

Method....move the fabric smoothly in any direction, creating stitches of an acceptable and even length. Practice writing your name and address in 'joined up 'writing to gain control.

Jig Saw puzzling/Vermicelli Work

Useful for providing texture in large areas.... filling spaces.... creating colour in spaces..... or colouring cords if pattern is reduced in size.

Machine set as for free straight stitch, noting that it is much easier to get a rhythm going to create an even stitching pattern if the machine is running at a moderately fast, steady speed.

Method.... move fabric smoothly in small half circular swings....do not cross any sewn lines.... keep spaces even in size. The best effect is achieved when used as a quilting stitch where texture is required.

'Peaky' Straight Stitch: useful for outlining ' flower style' centres in designs... substituting for irregular zig zag in confined spaces.

Machine set as for free straight stitch

Method..... with machine running quite fast, move the fabric backwards and forwards or from side to side as required with sharp changes of direction creating 'peaks' of different lengths. Each peak contains a varying number of stitches.

Blind Hemstitch: useful for high class invisible appliqué often mistaken for hand stitching if well done using invisible thread.

```
Machine set as follows.....
selected stitch...... ---^---^---^-
stitch width ......... between 1/2 and 1
stitch length ........ between 1/2 and 1
feed dog ............... engaged
machine foot ....... normal
speed ................... as comfortable
NB
Needle position .. CENTRAL
```

Method..... follow bias edge, sewing the straight stitches on the background fabric and the tiny intermittent zigzag on the bias. Use transparent thread in the needle. The bottom thread should match the background fabric.

Machine Set Decorative Stitches:
useful for filter stitches.... and decorative contour quilting.

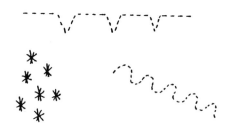

```
Machine set as follows.......
selected stitch... chosen stitch
stitch width ...... medium to wide
stitch length ..... optional
feed dog ........... engaged
machine foot .... normal
speed ................ as comfortable
```

Method..... allow fabric to feed through machine without pushing. Check if your machine provides a visual guide when the start of a repeat is reached, or if it is possible to do one repeat at a time for small filler stitches.

A Few Points

1. Remember that if the preceding stitches are used to quilt at the same time as embroider, they will show the stitching on the reverse side of the work. This may, or may not be acceptable.

2. Areas of quilting, which are heavily worked become a little hard to the touch. Embroidering the single fabric before quilting eliminates this problem.

3. The quality of embroidery is often improved by machine stitching over a stabilizer placed under the fabric. If this can be removed the work will not be stiff. Paper is useful for this since it can be mostly torn or soaked away, and for me is therefore preferable to other stabilizers. This can only be used with single fabric.

4. To aid even stitching, it helps to place a thick book behind the machine pedal. The thickness should correspond to the level the pedal depresses to when your machine is running at your chosen speed. This enables the speed be constantly achieved and maintained, since your toe presses to touch the book and no further.

Bias Appliqué

Since very detailed instructions for this technique appear in my previous book 'Sew Easy Celtic', a shortened version is now provided.

Estimating Fabric Requirements

1. To clarify the bias requirement for a single cord, lay a length of wool around the cord on a single design slice. Multiply this length by the number of sections included and add a little extra for luck.

2. To estimate the bias yield from a given sized fabric square follow this table. Bias is calculated at 1in wide and is therefore suitable for several of the narrower width bias bars.

Square	Bias	Square	Bias
8in	50in	15in	200in
9in	72in	16½in	242in
10½in	98in	17½in	288in
12in	128in	19in	338in
13½in	162in	20½in	392in

Cutting Fabric at 45 degrees

1. Having decided on the size square of fabric required, use the 45 degree angle marked on rotary rulers to cut the square diagonally on the bias.

2. Flip all the resulting cut triangles on top of each other. If using striped fabric check all fabric is right side up and all stripes run in the same direction.

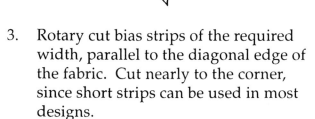

3. Rotary cut bias strips of the required width, parallel to the diagonal edge of the fabric. Cut nearly to the corner, since short strips can be used in most designs.

Sewing Bias into Tubes

1. Fold fabric strips in half lengthwise.... right side out.

2. Place a flat sided magnet by the side of the machine foot to prevent the tube from altering its position as it is sewn. The distance from the needle to the magnet should equal the size of the bias bar being used.

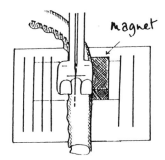

3. Place the fabric fold next to the magnet and sew along tube's length using a very short stitch length..... having double checked at the start that the bias bar can fit snugly inside the sewn tube.

4. Sew all strips 'factory style'.... sewing the end of one to the start of the next....don't worry if the join is messy, as it will be removed.

5. If sewing mixed colours in bias fabric sew different colours in turn to make the joins clearly visible.

6. Cut off pointed ends and cut out all joins.

7. Cut surplus seam allowance from all tubes to approximately 1/16 in from stitches.

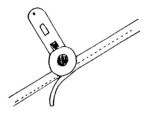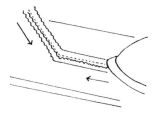

8. Press dampened tubes flat, with the seam at centre back, by slipping the bias bar inside and gently feeding the fabric tube off at one end, to be immediately ironed. The seam allowance is pressed to one side, if it flips over to the other it does not matter since it is so small.

Preparing to Appliqué

Perfect machine appliqué of Celtic designs needs Bondaweb™ fusible webbing to hold the cords in place until they are sewn down.

Bondaweb™ Tips

1. Always buy from a roll .... never packets to lessen its tendency to separate from its backing paper.

2. Reject battered webbing already separating.

3. Request the shop to roll, not fold it.

4. Remove the plastic 'ideas' insert.

5. Heat the rolled webbing.... paper side out, with your iron to increase adhesion of webbing to paper.

6. Do not unroll while still sticky. Place in a freezer for a few minutes if you are in a hurry. It will unroll when cold.

7. Rotary cut webbing into strips which match the bias tube width. Place the webbing, paper side down on the cutting board. Cut only one or two strips at a time.

8. Iron the webbing to the seam side of all pressed fabric tubes. Remove the paper.

9. Iron the prepared tubes in place on your marked fabric... the webbing will hold them in position.

10. Start and finish all tubes at an 'under' intersection in the design. Butt cord ends together... they will be covered by the 'over' cord.

11. Follow and complete one cord at a time.

12. Apply a little tension to the fabric tube when ironing it around tight curves.

13. Create points by folding a little tuck in the tube.

14. 'Over' cords can be stuck on top.... while 'unders' can be created by lifting a little 'bridge' in an already stuck down cord. Pass the under cord through and re-stick.

Stitching for Appliqué

1. Choose from the three stitching alternatives:

   Straight stitch P24
   Zig zag P24
   Blind Hemstitch P26

2. Sew both edges of all tubes.... also through 'tucks' forming points, using transparent thread.

3. Lift the presser foot and 'jump' across 'over' cords doing a few stitches on the spot on both sides of the 'jump' to lock the thread. This is not necessary with blind hemstitch.

4. Snip off all loops created by the 'jumps' on the right side of the work.

Adding Coloured Fabric Inserts

There are two methods of adding inserts. Both are completed **BEFORE** placing the bias.

Method A.....

1. Trace the space you wish to fill on greaseproof paper. The embroidery transfer pencil lines mark the outer limit of any space.

2. Using the greaseproof paper as a template cut the insert from the chosen fabric.

3. Anchor the insert in the correct position, by pinning or sparing use of a glue stick.

4. The raw edges of the fabric will be covered by the appliqué of the bias cords.

Method B.......

Use this method if you do not wish to have double fabric in the inserts.

1. Cut out the centre of the space to be coloured, leaving 1/8in margin inside the transferred line.

2. Cut only one hole at a time and complete the insert before attempting another.

3. Lay a suitably sized piece of coloured fabric under the hole ..... with the right side of both fabrics facing upwards. Anchor it in place with pins or glue stick.

4. On the right side of the design, free machine straight stitch around the cut out shape. Sew exactly on the transferred line, using very short stitches to provide stability.

5. Trim the reverse side edges of the inserted fabric to 1/4in.

6. Apply and sew bias strips as usual. The appliqué stitch will further stabilize the cut fabric.

BIBLIOGRAPHY

DAVIS, COURTNEY .... 'Celtic Borders and Decoration' .... BLANDFORD 1992

BAIN, IAIN .... 'Celtic Knotwork' .... CONSTABLE 1986

BAIN, GEORGE .... Celtic Art, the Methods of Construction .... CONSTABLE 1951

HARGRAVE, HARRIET .... Mastering Machine Appliqué .... C. T. PUBLISHING 1991

LAING LLOYD .... Later Celtic Art .... SHIRE ARCHAEOLOGY 1987

MEGAW, RUTH & VINCENT .. Early Celtic Art .... SHIRE ARCHAEOLOGY 1986

MEGAW, RUTH & VINCENT .. Celtic Art from its beginnings
                                                    to the Book of Kells .... THAMES AND HUDSON 1989

WIECHEC, PHILOMENA .... Celtic Quilt Designs .... CELTIC DESIGN CO. 1980

MADDEN, ANGELA .... Sew Easy Celtic M.C.Q.1993

Design Placement Guide

Fairy Ring Design Pattern Slice
(6 slice design)

Celtic Tranquility Design Pattern Slice
5 slice design

32

Spinning Star Design Pattern Slice
5 slice design

Forest Flower Design Pattern Slice
6 slice design